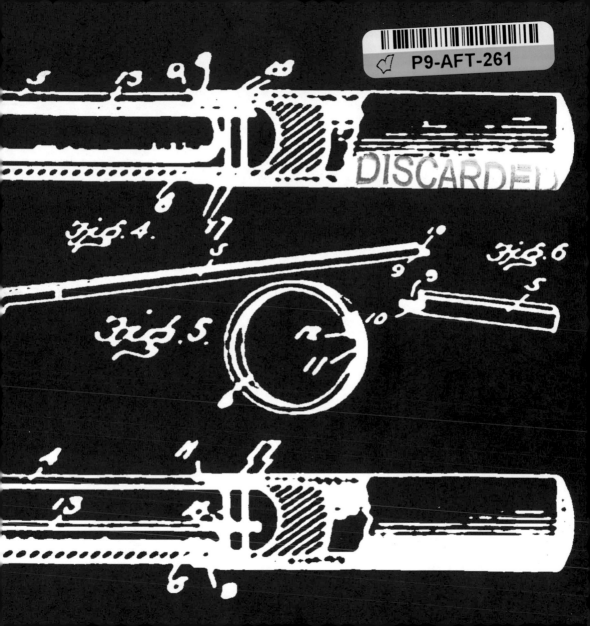

THE
PEN

THE

PEN

AN APPRECIATION

AURUM PRESS

DAVID ATTWOOD ⊙ PHOTOGRAPHS BY GUY RYECART

First published in Great Britain 1998 by
Aurum Press Limited
25 Bedford Avenue
London WC1B 2AT

A catalogue record for this book is
available from the British Library

ISBN 1 85410 595 7

This book was conceived,
designed and produced by
THE IVY PRESS LIMITED
2/3 St Andrews Place
Lewes, East Sussex
BN7 1UP

Art Director: *Peter Bridgewater*
Editorial Director: *Sophie Collins*
Managing Editor: *Anne Townley*
Project Editor: *Caroline Earle*
Editor: *Julie Whitaker*
Designer: *Ron Bryant-Funnell*
Photography: *Guy Ryecart*

Printed and bound in China

Throughout this book the length of the
pens are given in imperial and metric
measurements.

22

15

12

15

23

29

25

20

11

24

29

31

16

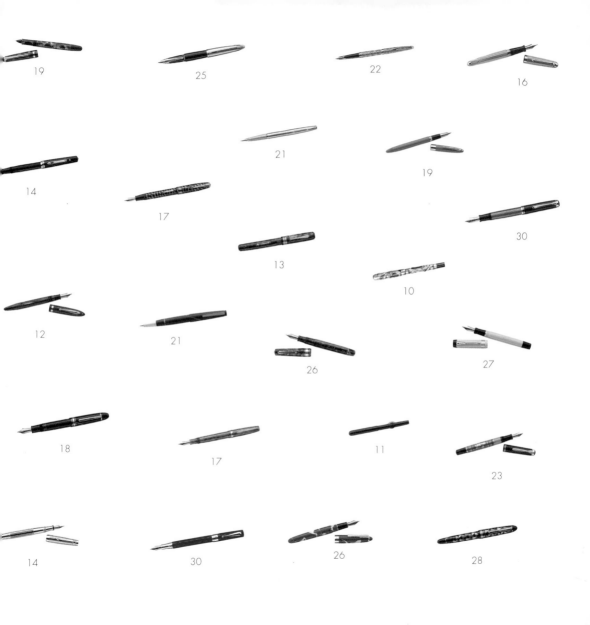

19

25

22

16

21

19

14

17

30

13

10

12

21

26

27

18

17

11

23

14

30

26

28

Introduction

Most of us have any number of cheap and anonymous pens lying around, and 30 or 40 years ago the eponymous 'Biro', so cheap and convenient, seemed to have driven out the old-fashioned fountain pen for good. However, with the design conscious 1980s came a renewed demand for the pen as a luxury object.

'Big Red' Duofold
Parker, 1922

Nowadays collectors snap up vintage models, while makers revive old pens or create new ones in precious limited editions.

Patrician
Waterman
c1930

Whatever the product, manufacturers have always seen differentiation as a means of expanding the market, and pens are no exception. A pen can be a very personal thing. High-tech modern or nostalgic traditional, small and feminine or oversized status symbol, the pens people choose say a lot about how they see themselves.

From the early Middle Ages, people wrote with quill pens – made from the feathers of geese or other birds. Quills weren't replaced by metal pens and nibs until the mid-19th century but such pens still had to be dipped in ink every few words. Many people tried to invent a pen with a built-in ink supply that also (more difficult) fed ink evenly to the nib without blotting. The English inventor Joseph Bramah patented a capillary nib feed in 1809; New Yorker L. E. Waterman

Doric
Wahl Eversharp, c1931

perfected and re-patented it in 1884, and made his fortune.

By this time, some pens were works of art in themselves, fashioned from chased or filigreed gold or silver. Most, though, were made from the hard rubber (ebonite) patented by Goodyear in 1851. Nibs were of gold or steel, tipped with rare hard metals such as iridium.

Turn of the century fountain pens had to be filled with a messy 'eyedropper' but 'safety' pens that wouldn't leak into your pocket or bag were popular. From around 1904, makers came up with ingenious ways of compressing a thin rubber sac inside the pen barrel that could then be released to suck up ink from a bottle. Parker's press-button filler and Sheaffer's side

Sheaffer
Snorkel Nib Detail, c1952

Aurora 88
Marcello Nizzoli 1947/1990

lever filler brought both companies success after the First World War, and the side lever was widely used well into the 1950s. Parker, Sheaffer and Waterman made up the 'big three' pen manufacturers for much of the century; all three started in small workshops and grew to international stature.

The 1920s was the heyday of the fountain pen. At the start of the decade most pens were still made of ebonite, generally black though sometimes mottled. In 1921 Parker caused a stir with their 'Big Red' Duofold: its shape was widely influential and still looks fashionable today. Sheaffer was the first to use celluloid plastic in 1924 and other makers soon followed, offering beautiful marbled effects as well as a wider range of colours. The end of the 1920s brought Art Deco detailing, and pens grew more tapered as they picked up the fashionable streamlined styling. The big US brands spread around the world, but successful pens were made in Europe too – Onoto and Swan in Britain, Aurora and Omas in Italy, Pelikan and Montblanc in Germany. Meanwhile, Japan began a tradition of exquisitely decorated lacquered pens.

In the 1920s and 1930s makers vied to come up with new designs and marketing stunts. There was a fashion for pens with a visible ink supply, and another for 'lifetime' guarantees to entice buyers during the Depression. Then

Sailor Profit 80
Detail, 1991

came the world's best-selling pen, the Parker 51, launched in 1941 after a long development programme. Its sleek shell and hooded nib were picked up by other pen designers in the 1940s.

Laslo Biro's 1938 ball-point patent, however, almost killed off the fountain pen altogether. Early ball-points were expensive and unreliable, but prices soon fell. Several smaller fountain pen makers went out of business, while larger ones had to come up with new features and designs to compete. At the end of the 1950s, cheap disposable

Aurora Cellini
Detail, 1997

products such as the French Bic helped to seal the ball-point's domination. Prestige pen makers survived, however, adding matching ball-points and then roller-balls to their ranges alongside the fountain pens and propelling pencils. From the 1960s, Italian and German makers commissioned famous designers to fashion exciting new styles in stainless steel or matt black. Today, pens such as these share the stage with intricate, beautiful limited editions that recall the fountain pen's golden age.

SILVER ON HARD RUBBER, 1905, 5IN / 13CM

PARKER 'SNAKE'

George Parker taught telegraphy 1880s Wisconsin and at first sold pens only as a sideline. But from 1889 he came up with a string of patents that literally transformed the pen industry. One was the 'Lucky Curve' ink feed of 1894 that helped prevent a pen from leaking in your jacket pocket. Some early Parkers used finely decorated gold or silver, and 'snake' pens, such as this one, which originally cost just eight dollars, are particularly rare and valuable.

WATERMAN IDEAL

L ewis Edson Waterman began his career selling insurance in New York. Like George Parker he sold pens too. The story goes that he lost important business when a leaky pen ruined a document, and set out to find a better one. His patent for an improved ink feed paved the way for the modern fountain pen. But pens of the time still had to be filled with a messy 'eyedropper' – self-filling pens came later.

GOLD-FILLED FILIGREE ON HARD RUBBER, 1910s, 5.5IN / 14CM

CONKLIN CRESCENT FILLER

A n inventor in Toledo, Ohio, Roy Conklin developed the first practical self-filling pen in 1897. The 'crescent'-shaped piece on the side of the pen squeezes a rubber ink sac inside when pressed; when released, ink is drawn into the sac. The company prospered, and by the 1910s Conklin's invention had become the top-selling self-filler pen.

HARD RUBBER, 1910s, 5IN / 13CM

CELLULOID, 1930s, 5.5IN / 1

PARKER 'BIG RED' DUOFOLD

Around 1920, when most low-priced pens were still manufactured in black or mottled ebonite, Parker introduced a new large pen in a striking orange-red colour. Initially greeted with scepticism, the Duofold (so-called because it originally came with a barrel extension for use as either a pocket or a desk pen) was hugely successful. Later Duofolds were plastic, but the shape and style of the classic 'Big Red' has influenced pen design to this day.

SHEAFFER LIFETIME

In 1908 Walter Sheaffer, a jeweller by trade, patented the side-lever filler that was to be widely used for the next 50 years. This 'Lifetime' pen had a nib guaranteed as long as the owner lived and a 'balanced' shape to sit easily in the hand. Sheaffer was also first with plastic pens in 1924. Celluloid and similar plastics opened up a whole new range of colours and patterns. The famous Sheaffer white dot trademark also dates from this time.

HARD RUBBER, 1922, 6IN / 15CM

WATERMAN
PATRICIAN

Waterman were slow to introduce plastic pens and by the end of the 1920s they lagged behind other makers in terms of style. Then came the Patrician, now acknowledged as one of the classic Art Deco pens. The cap ring, in particular, has fine detailing. It was available in black or five colours of beautifully marbled plastic.

CELLULOID, c1930, 5.5IN / 14CM

WAHL EVERSHARP DORIC

In 1915 the Wahl Adding Machine Co bought a stake in Eversharp propelling pencils and soon after that began designing a successful range of pens. Although they were pioneers in modern mass production methods, they didn't introduce a plastic pen until 1929. Their Gold Seal models followed the Art Deco trend among pen designs and the more streamlined Doric was a favourite of the 1930s.

CELLULOID, c1931, 6IN / 15CM

GOLD PLATE, c1935, 5.5IN / 14CM

SWAN LEVERLESS

In 1884 the American Mabie Todd company opened a London office that imported eyedropper pens. By the turn of the century the brand name 'Swan' was synonymous with the fountain pen. The British arm flourished, and in 1915 took over the US business. While their pens weren't particularly innovative, they dominated the UK market between the wars. This 1930s leverless pen is filled by twisting a knob at the end of the barrel.

PARKER VACUMATIC

The Depression marked a downturn in consumer spending and the pen market needed that something extra to encourage people to buy. Parker spent five years perfecting the Vacuum Filler, later called the Vacumatic, for its Duofold range. With its large ink capacity and visible ink supply (made by using a laminated plastic barrel) it was an immediate success in 1933 and much copied by other makers. The now-famous arrow clip also made its first appearance here.

CELLULOID, 1930s, 5 in / 13 cm

ONOTO

The British company Thomas De La Rue built a printing empire in the 19th century producing stamps, bank notes and playing cards; and in 1880 it produced its first pen. De La Rue bought a patent for a plunger self-filling mechanism and launched the Onoto pen around 1905, apparently choosing the name as suitable for export since it was acceptable in many languages.

CELLULOID, c1948, 5.5IN / 14CM

PARKER 51

Revolutionary and influential, the Parker 51 had a sleek streamlined shell and hooded nib. Launched in 1941, the 51 cost Parker a phenomenal quarter of a million dollars to develop, but it was money well spent – they went on to sell 41 million of them. At the same time Parker also came up with a new, quick drying ink. At first the 51 used the Vacumatic fill, but in 1948 the simpler Aeromatic system was introduced, which merely had to be squeezed between finger and thumb.

AURORA 88
MARCELLO NIZZOLI

Like many European companies, the early pens of the Italian manufacturer Aurora were heavily influenced by US designs. This 88 design was the work of Milanese designer Marcello Nizzoli, famed for his now-classic typewriter designs for Olivetti. Originally it had a hooded nib such as that of the popular Parker 51. The 88 was extremely successful, and it is still in vogue 50 years later, though now (as here) it has the more traditional looking open nib.

GOLD PLATE, 1947/1990, 5.5IN / 14CM

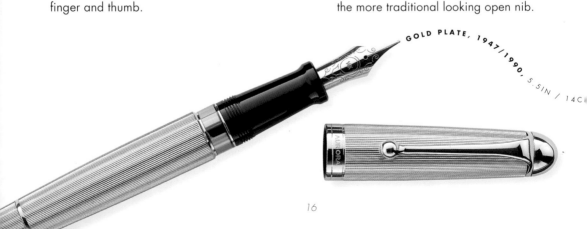

CELLULOID, c1951, 5.5IN / 14CM

CONWAY STEWART NO. 58

Two popular music hall entertainers of the 1900s are thought to have given the Conway Stewart company its name. Whatever its origin, the company was well known for making good-quality, low-cost pens throughout the 1920s and 1930s. The pens came in a wide range of lustrous colours, but this black and white 'cracked ice' finish is unique to the company. Lasting well into the 1950s, the Conway Stewart name brings back many inky-fingered memories for a whole generation of British schoolchildren.

SOENNECKEN 222

German company Soennecken started off making stationery, and invented the ring binder and hole punch. In the 1890s they diversified and became the first of the great German fountain pen makers. Sales boomed both at home and abroad during the 1920s and 1930s, and business recovered after the Second World War. This attractive lizard finish pen dates from 1952 but soon thereafter competition from ball-points sent Soennecken on a downhill spiral from which it never recovered.

CELLULOID, c1952, 5.5IN / 14CM

MONTBLANC
MEISTERSTUCK 149

The German Simplo company's early 'Rouge et Noir' pens had a black cap topped with a red disc. Around 1910 they introduced white-topped pens that came to be known as Mont Blanc – after the Alpine mountain – and from this their famous white star logo developed. Montblanc launched their top of the range 'Meisterstuck' or Masterpiece pens in 1924. The height of Mont Blanc (in metres) came to be engraved on the cap and later on the nib – as it still is today. The large 149 pen gained new cult status in the 1980s.

PLASTIC, 1952, 6.5IN / 17CM

PLASTIC, c1952, 5.5IN / 14CM

SHEAFFER VALIANT

After the war Sheaffer worked hard to develop new filling systems that could compete with the easy to use ball-point. New designs such as the Touchdown of 1949 helped keep them at the top of the industry. Then in 1952 came the innovative Snorkel, named after the underwater air supply used by submarines. When filling the pen, a fine tube emerged beneath the nib to suck up ink, keeping the nib itself clean.

ROTRING STYLOGRAPH

The Stylograph was a technical drawing pen with a fine metal tube instead of a gold nib. A plus point was that it could make carbon copies. By the mid-1930s they were widely exported. The German company wasn't actually known as Rotring until much later; the name came from this 1950s Rapidograph model that had a distinctive red (German: *rot*) ring in the barrel. Rotring still make a range of high-tech drawing and fountain pens.

CELLULOID, c1956, 5IN / 13CM

PARKER 75

Launched to mark the 75th anniversary of the company, the 75 had a contoured grip and adjustable nib that could be turned to suit different writing styles. It stayed in production for almost 40 years in a wide range of finishes, but this distinctive Ciselé (cross-hatched) design in sterling silver or vermeil (gilded silver) is one of the most collectable.

PLASTIC AND STEEL, 1966, 5.5IN / 14CM

STAINLESS STEEL, 1970s, 5.5IN / 14CM

LAMY 2000

GERD A MULLER

Josef Lamy worked for Parker before founding his own company in 1930. His early pens were influenced (as were so many other German makes) by the Duofold. By the 1960s Lamy felt the need for a totally new design. He brought in Bauhaus-influenced designer Gerd A Muller who created the Lamy 2000. With its high-tech textured steel and plastic finish, the 2000 proved a popular and stylish design and has been in production ever since. Lamy has a tradition of using noted designers: their Persona pen was designed by Mario Bellini.

PARKER FALCON

In 1970 Parker launched the space-age T1. Made almost entirely of titanium, the nib formed part of the barrel. However, as titanium is so hard, the pen proved difficult to make and was discontinued after a year. Parker came back with the similar-looking Falcon, the second pen in history without a separate nib – the first being the quill!

PENTEL R50

PLASTIC, 1970s, 5.5IN / 14CM

Any colour you like, so long as it is green – the R50 has been described as the Model T Ford of writing instruments. It has the same iconic qualities – mass produced, value for money and made in one instantly recognizable colour. Pentel produced their first fibre-tip pen in 1960, but it was the R50 roller-ball that really made their name.

WATERMAN CF

A pen that could be filled by simply slipping in a new ink cartridge had been tried over the years but didn't really take off until Waterman launched their CF (cartridge filler) model in 1953. Now extremely popular, most cartridge pens come with a converter for filling them from the traditional ink bottle. This Waterman came in several distinctively patterned gold-plated finishes including this unusual crocodile pattern.

GOLD PLATE, c1976, 5.5IN / 14CM

SHEAFFER TARGA

'BLUE RONCE' LACQUER, 1976, 6IN / 15CM

By the mid-1970s the public in Europe and the USA was beginning to show renewed interest in high-quality fountain pens. The Targa, introduced in 1976, gained prestige from being named after the Targa Florio motor race held in Sicily. It had a gold inlaid nib and finishes including engine-turned gold or silver.

PLASTIC, SILVER AND GOLD, 1989, 5IN / 13CM

PELIKAN TOLEDO 700

Pelikan was a long-established German company making inks, paints and stationery before launching its first pen in 1925. Dating from 1935 the Toledo design is characterized by a special technique that involves plating a silver sleeve on the barrel with gold. An ornate scene featuring pelican motifs is then etched by hand onto the barrel. As with other Pelikans, the pocket clip is in the shape of a pelican's beak.

SAILOR PROFIT 80

The brush and ink stick were once the accepted means of writing in Japan, but fountain pens became popular from the early 1900s. The Sailor company was formed in 1911, taking its name from a nearby naval base. Since 1968 Sailor has made wooden pens. Some are richly decorated with Maki-E designs; others simply celebrate the beauty of wood. This limited edition marked the company's 80th anniversary.

WATERMAN EDSON

Named after the company's founder, Lewis Edson Waterman, the Edson has a double-walled barrel giving it a unique depth of colour. The nib resembles the prow of a ship, the cap is in satin gold and each pen is engraved with a personal number. A special hood over the ink feed is claimed to prevent leakage at high altitudes.

PILOT MAKI-E

Pilot was formed in 1918. In 1925, one of its founders, Ruyosuke Namiki, had the idea of decorating lacquered pens with traditional Japanese subjects. They used gold and silver dust and other precious materials – the ancient craft called Maki-E. In the 1930s London luxury goods maker Alfred Dunhill reached an agreement to sell their pens under the Dunhill-Namiki name.

DECORATED LACQUER, 1994, 5.5IN / 14CM

RECIFE MYSTIQUE

Recife is a new and fairly small company making low-priced high-fashion pens from a range of unusual materials. They have even resurrected ebonite – the hard rubber material that has been little used in pen production since celluloid plastics replaced it in the 1920s. Mystique is a plastic exclusive to this French company. Recife have also created 'Andy Warhol' limited editions that pick up the colours and patterns from the artist's celebrated screen prints.

PLASTIC, 1990s, 6IN / 15CM

OMAS EXTRA

Around 1919 the Omas company was just a small pen parts workshop in Bologna, Italy, but it grew to become a pen maker in its own right. The company developed special tools to cut the faceted barrels that became something of an Omas trademark; this is a modern example. Intriguing and innovative vintage Omas pens include the 'Doctor's Pen' that came complete with a handy clinical thermometer in the barrel, and the 'Zerolo' that had two separate nibs for different ink colours.

CELLULOID, 1994, 5.5IN / 14CM

PARKER DUOFOLD CENTENNIAL

The Lucky Curve Duofold of the early 1920s was enormously influential. Early ebonite Duofolds were followed by celluloid versions in other colours. George Parker brought out a 'mandarin yellow' version after being fascinated by the colour of a cloisonné vase while on a business trip to the Far East. This is the new limited edition Duofold that Parker brought out in 1995.

PLATINUM
MAKI-E

Platinum began by importing pens to Japan from the West early this century, but started making their own pens in the 1920s and named their company after the precious metal. They launched Maki-E lacquer pens in the 1930s, and are still renowned for them today. This geometric pattern is based on traditional kimono textile designs. In the 1960s and 1970s, Platinum brought out leather pens covered in the skins of reptiles such as snake, lizard and crocodile.

DECORATED LACQUER, 1996, 6IN / 15CM

PLASTIC, 1990s, 6.5IN / 17CM

OMAS TOKYO
ETTORE SOTTSASS

Another Italian designer who has worked for Olivetti, Ettore Sottsass is a key figure in 20th-century design. From the 1960s onward, he was involved in radical 'anti-design' groups that challenged the accepted modernist wisdom of functional good taste, leading up to the 'Memphis' group's often outrageous post-modern furniture of the 1980s. By contrast, his Tokyo pen for Omas is on clean and simple modern lines.

AURORA CELLINI

The Aurora Cellini pen is a limited edition, cast in solid sterling silver by the 'lost wax' process. It was named in honour of the great Florentine Renaissance artist Benvenuto Cellini (1500–1571), who worked as a goldsmith and sculptor in Italy and France. Aurora limited edition pens are popular with collectors.

Another beautiful example is the Dante Alighieri, released in 1994 to mark the company's 75th anniversary.

SILVER, 1997, 6.5IN / 16CM

PELIKAN 1000

In 1929 Pelikan launched a patented piston filling system which was very successful. The piston filler was adopted and is still used by Montblanc today. This recent Pelikan has the pelican beak clip and the classic green and black striped finish typical of Pelikan pens since the early 1950s.

PLASTIC, 1997, 6.5IN / 16CM

MONTEGRAPPA SYMPHONY

Italy's first fountain pen maker was founded in 1912 in Bassano del Grappa, north-west of Venice, where it still flourishes today. It pioneered the manufacture of celluloid pens. Celluloid, however, is highly flammable and, after a disastrous factory fire in 1946, Montegrappa switched to precious metals. The Symphony range marks a return to their classic celluloid pens.

CELLULOID, 1997, 6.5IN / 16CM

METAL AND PLASTIC, 1997, 5IN / 13CM

STYPEN HARLEY DAVIDSON

Born to be wild? Leather-clad bikers and fountain pens may seem strange partners, but if a brand image is powerful enough it knows no bounds. The iconography of one product – and the Harley dream machine must be the ultimate American icon – can make another quite different one more desirable.

ACKNOWLEDGEMENTS

The publishers would particularly like
to thank the following for use of pictures
and loan of pens:

**Andreas Lambrou, Classic Pens
Ltd:** 12 left and right; 14 right; 15 left
and right; 16 left and right; 17 left and
right; 18; 19 left and right; 20; 21 right;
22 bottom; 23 top and bottom; 24; 25
left and right; 26 top and bottom; 27; 28;
29 right; 30 left and right

**Simon Gray, Battersea Pens
Home:** 11 left and right; 13; 14 left

**Bridgeman Art Library/
Bonhams:** 10

GBA Pen Co: 29 left

The Pen Shop: 21 left

Sheaffer Pen UK Ltd: endpapers (W.
A. Sheaffer's original patent for a lever self-
filling fountain pen)

Stypen (UK) Ltd: 31

Thanks also to **Trevor Russell**

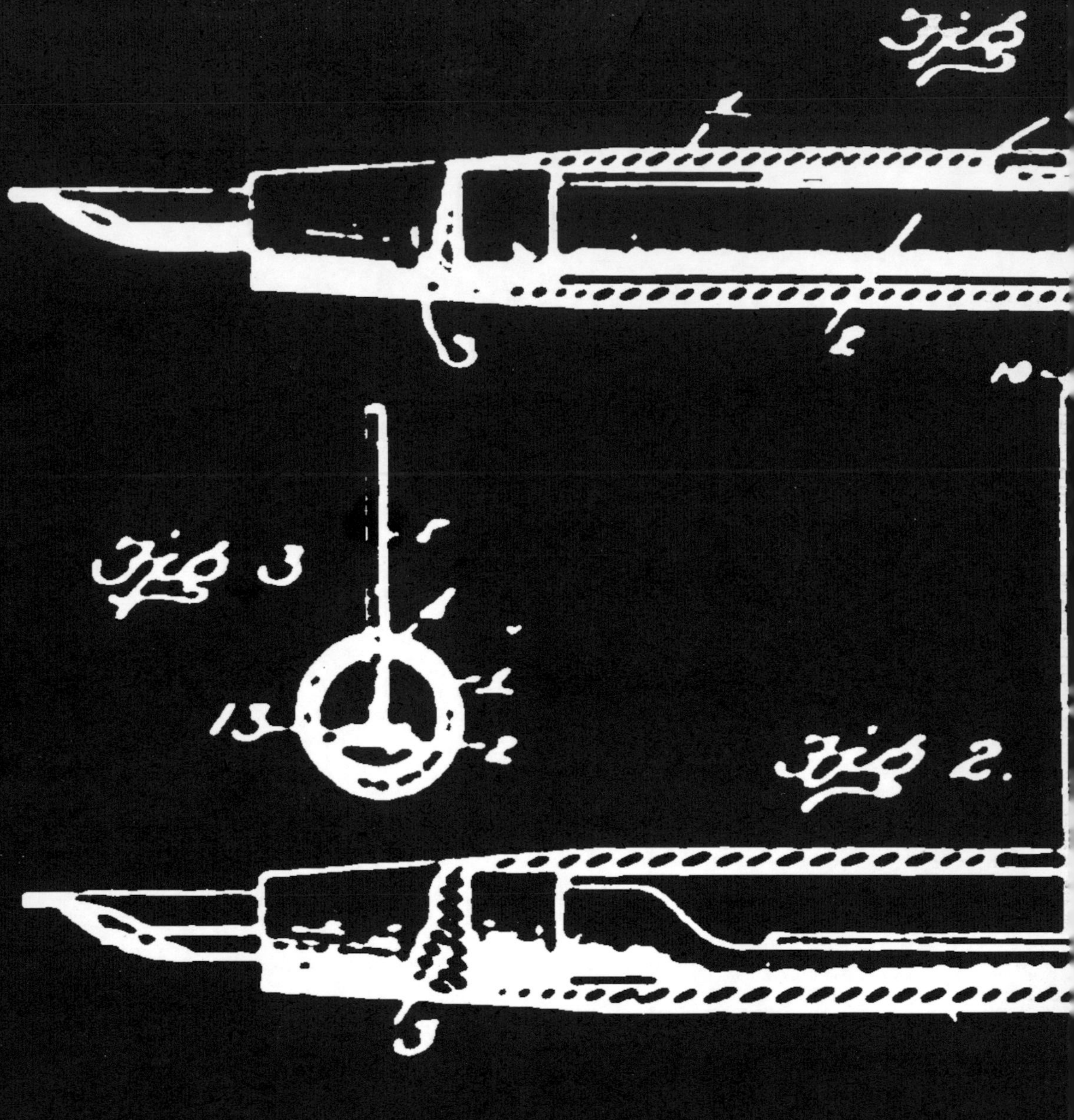

Fig. 1

Fig. 3

Fig. 2

13